CREATIVE EDUCATION

EARLY SPORTS BOOKS

MEET THE DEFENSEMEN

by Linda Thomas

photographs from the National Hockey League

creative education
childrens press

Published by Creative Educational Society, Inc., 123 South Broad Street, Mankato, Minnesota 56001 Copyright © 1976 by Creative Educational Society, Inc. International copyrights reserved in all countries. No part of this book may be reproduced in any form without written permission from the publisher. Printed in the United States.

Library of Congress Cataloging in Publication Data
Thomas, Linda   Meet the defensemen.
SUMMARY: Biographical sketches of four hockey deflense-
men: Brad Parks, Ed Van Impe, Bobby Orr, and Denis Potvin.
1. Hockey—Biography—Juvenile literature.
[1. Hockey—Biography]   I. Title.
GV848.5.A1M635   796.9'62'0922 [B]   [920]   76-24912
ISBN 0-87191-535-9

BRAD PARK

Brad Park started in the National Hockey League during the 1968-69 season. This was quite a year to play in the NHL. The top scorers in the NHL that season included Phil Esposito, Gordie Howe, Bobby Hull and Bobby Orr.

Brad finished his rookie year for the New York Rangers with 3 goals and 23 assists.

In his second season, Brad made the All-Star team.
He had completed the year with 11 goals and 26
assists. The other members of the All-Star team were
Phil and Tony Esposito, Gordie Howe, Bobby Hull and
Bobby Orr.

During the 1970-71 season, Brad finished with
7 goals and 37 assists. He again made the All-Star
team. But the Rangers were eliminated by the Chicago
Black-Hawks in the play-offs. It took seven games,
three of which went into overtime, before the
Rangers fell.

SHER-WooD

In the 1971-72 season, the Bruins took first place in
the East Division. They finished 10 points ahead of
the Rangers. So the Rangers were again the number
two team in the East Division. Again, Brad made the
All-Star team. He also set a Ranger record for a
defenseman. He made 24 goals and 49 assists. This
was only the third time in NHL history that a defenseman had scored 20 or more goals in one season.

Brad was out with a knee injury during most of the
1972-73 season. He missed 26 games. Still he was able
to finish the season with 10 goals and 43 assists.

The top scorer for the New York Rangers during the 1973-74 season was defenseman Brad Park. He had a total of 82 points. The Rangers also came very close to the Stanley Cup Finals. They lost in the semi-finals to the Philadelphia Flyers.

The Rangers made Brad their team captain for the 1974-75 season. Then at the end of the season Brad was traded to the Boston Bruins.

The 1975-76 season with the Bruins found Brad out most of the time with a knee injury. Brad Park is still listed as one of the best defensemen in the National Hockey League.

Ed Van Impe did not join the National Hockey League until the 1966-67 season. He was a rookie for the Chicago Black Hawks. It was a great season! Chicago was number one in the NHL.

Ed finished second in the contest for Rookie of the Year. The winner of the award was Bobby Orr.

The NHL added six new teams on June 6, 1967. The new teams drafted players from the established teams. One of the new teams, the Philadelphia Flyers, drafted Ed Van Impe.

The Flyers completed their first year by being first in the West Division. They also elected Ed as their captain that year. Then in the next two seasons the Flyers fell to third and fifth places.

Ed had not felt comfortable as the team leader. So in 1971 Bobby Clarke took over as the Captain. The Flyers finished in second place in the West Division during the 1972-73 season.

The 1973-74 season was the year for the Philadelphia Flyers. They finished in first place in the West Division. The Flyers also won the Stanley Cup.

The Flyers were back strong again in the 1974-75 season. They again won the first place spot in the West Division and the Stanley Cup.

In the 1975-76 season the Flyers lost the Stanley Cup to the Montreal Canadiens. Although most of the credit for the success of the Flyers goes to other players like Bobby Clarke or Bernie Parent, Ed Van Impe is a very important part of the Philadelphia Flyers.

Bobby Orr is the superstar of hockey's defensemen.

Bobby joined the Boston Bruins in the 1966-67 season. He won the Calder Trophy as Rookie of the Year. He finished with 13 goals and 28 assists. The Bruins finished in last place.

The Bruins moved to third place in the 1967-68 season. Bobby won the Norris Trophy as the top defenseman in the National Hockey League! He had made 11 goals and 20 assists.

A new record for defensemen was set by Bobby
during the 1968-69 season. He made 21 goals and 43
assists. Again he won the Norris Trophy. The Bruins
moved up to second place.

The 1969-70 season was quite a year for Bobby Orr
and the Boston Bruins. Bobby was elected Captain
for the Bruins. He was the leading scorer in the NHL.
He made 33 goals and 87 assists. It was the first time
in NHL history that a defenseman was the top scorer.
He won the Norris Trophy, the Ross Trophy as leading
scorer and the Hart Trophy as Most Valuable Player.
The Boston Bruins won the Stanley Cup.

VICTORIA

In the 1973-74 season the Bruins lost the Stanley
Cup to the Philadelphia Flyers. It was an exciting
contest. And when it was over, the first player to
congratulate the winning Flyers was Bobby Orr.

During the last few years Bobby has not played much
because of knee injuries and operations. Still in the
1974-75 season he was the top scorer in the NHL. He
made 46 goals and 89 assists. Bobby was not able to
play in the 1975-76 season after November 26, 1975.
The records that he has already set make Bobby Orr
a legend.

DENIS POTVIN

Denis Potvin is one of the newest defensemen in the National Hockey League.

The New York Islanders added Denis to their team during the 1973-74 season. They finished that season in last place. Denis finished with 17 goals and 37 assists. This was a National Hockey League Record for total points by a rookie. He won the Calder Trophy as Rookie of the Year. It is only the second time that a defenseman has won this trophy in NHL history.

The Islanders moved up during the 1974-75 season.
They made it all the way to the semi-finals in the play-
offs. They were defeated by the Philadelphia Flyers.

Denis was listed as the number two defenseman in
the NHL. He was named to the All-Star team. Denis
Potvin was the top scorer for the Islanders. He made
21 goals and 55 assists.

The Islanders were defeated in the 1975-76 semi-
finals by the Montreal Canadiens. The Canadiens
went on to win the Stanley Cup. Denis has helped the
Islanders reach the semi-finals. And with Denis passing
the puck, the Islanders will probably soon win the
Stanley Cup. Denis Potvin may also become the next
superstar of hockey's defensemen.

CREATIVE EDUCATION

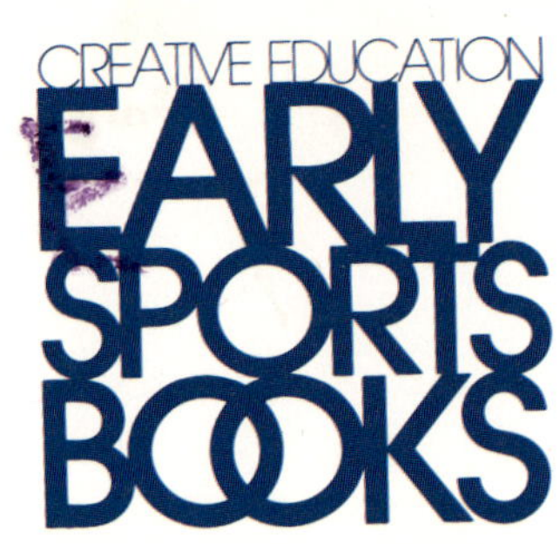

MEET THE COACHES
MEET THE LINEBACKERS
MEET THE RECEIVERS
MEET THE QUARTERBACKS
MEET THE RUNNING BACKS
MEET THE DEFENSIVE LINEMEN

MEET THE WINGMEN
MEET THE CENTERS
MEET THE DEFENSEMEN
MEET THE GOALIES

MEET THE INFIELDERS
MEET THE CATCHERS
MEET THE MANAGERS
MEET THE HITTERS
MEET THE PITCHERS